C000226005

THE ARDEN SHAKESPEARE
BOOK OF QUOTATIONS
ON

Death

Compiled by
JANE ARMSTRONG

AS

The Arden website is at
http://www.ardenshakespeare.com

First published 2001 by The Arden Shakespeare

This Collection Copyright © 2001 Jane Armstrong

Arden Shakespeare is an imprint of Thomson Learning

Thomson Learning
Berkshire House
168–173 High Holborn
London WC1V 7AA

Designed and typeset by Martin Bristow

Printed in Singapore by Seng Lee Press

British Library Cataloguing in Publication Data
A catalogue record for this book is available from the
British Library

Library of Congress Cataloguing in Publication Data
A catalogue record has been requested

ISBN 1-903436-53-2

NPN 9 8 7 6 5 4 3 2 1

Death

THE ARDEN SHAKESPEARE
BOOKS OF QUOTATIONS

Life

Love

Death

Nature

Songs & Sonnets

The Seven Ages of Man

Death

Death, that dark spirit.

Coriolanus 2.1.160

Finish, good lady. The bright day is done
And we are for the dark.

Antony and Cleopatra 5.2.192–3

I know when one is dead and when one lives;
She's dead as earth.

King Lear 5.3.258–9

A great reckoning in a little room.

As You Like It 3.3.14

Is this the promised end?

King Lear 5.3.261

Men must endure
Their going hence even as their coming hither.
Ripeness is all.

King Lear 5.2.9–11

An empty casket, where the jewel of life
By some damned hand was robbed and ta'en away.

King John 5.1.40–1

Barren rage of death's eternal cold.

Sonnet 13

[6]

This sight of death is as a bell
That warns my old age to a sepulchre.

Romeo and Juliet 5.3.206–7

The ripest fruit first falls, and so doth he;
His time is spent, our pilgrimage must be.

Richard II 2.1.153–4

This world's a city full of straying streets,
And death's the market-place where each one meets.

Two Noble Kinsmen 1.5.15–16

Hector is dead. There is no more to say.

Troilus and Cressida 5.11.22

'A parted even just between twelve and one, even at the turning o'th' tide. For after I saw him fumble with the sheets and play wi'th' flowers, and smile upon his fingers' ends, I knew there was but one way; for his nose was as sharp as a pen, and 'a babbled of green fields. 'How now, Sir John?' quoth I, 'what, man! be o' good cheer.' So 'a cried out 'God, God, God!' three or four times. Now I, to comfort him, bid him 'a should not think of God; I hoped there was no need to trouble himself with any such thoughts yet. So 'a bade me lay more clothes on his feet. I put my hand into the bed and felt them, and they were as cold as any stone. Then felt to his knees, and so up'ard, and up'ard, and all was as cold as any stone.

Henry V 2.3.12–25

He dies, and makes no sign.

2 Henry VI 3.3.29

Th' sure physician, Death.

Cymbeline 5.4.7

Vex not his ghost; O, let him pass. He hates him
That would upon the rack of this tough world
Stretch him out longer.

King Lear 5.3.312–14

Forbear to judge, for we are sinners all.
Close up his eyes, and draw the curtain close,
And let us all to meditation.

2 Henry VI 3.3.31–3

There is a willow grows askant the brook
That shows his hoary leaves in the glassy stream.
Therewith fantastic garlands did she make
Of crow-flowers, nettles, daisies, and long purples,
That liberal shepherds give a grosser name,
But our cold maids do dead men's fingers call them.
There on the pendent boughs her crownet weeds
Clamb'ring to hang, an envious sliver broke,
When down her weedy trophies and herself
Fell in the weeping brook. Her clothes spread wide,
And mermaid-like awhile they bore her up,
Which time she chanted snatches of old lauds,
As one incapable of her own distress,
Or like a creature native and indued
Unto that element. But long it could not be
Till that her garments, heavy with their drink,
Pulled the poor wretch from her melodious lay
To muddy death.

Hamlet 4.7.166–83

Sweets to the sweet. Farewell.

Hamlet 5.1.241

Death lies on her like an untimely frost
Upon the sweetest flower of all the field.

Romeo and Juliet 4.5.28–9

Cold, cold, my girl,
Even like thy chastity.

Othello 5.2.275–6

This fell sergeant, Death.

Hamlet 5.2.343

[11]

For God's sake let us sit upon the ground
And tell sad stories of the death of kings:
How some have been deposed, some slain in war,
Some haunted by the ghosts they have deposed,
Some poisoned by their wives, some sleeping killed,
All murthered – for within the hollow crown
That rounds the mortal temples of a king
Keeps Death his court, and there the antic sits,
Scoffing his state and grinning at his pomp,
Allowing him a breath, a little scene,
To monarchize, be feared, and kill with looks;
Infusing him with self and vain conceit,
As if this flesh which walls about our life
Were brass impregnable; and, humoured thus,
Comes at the last, and with a little pin
Bores thorough his castle wall, and farewell king!

Richard II 3.2.155–70

Death, as the Psalmist saith, is certain to all, all shall die.

2 Henry IV 3.2.38–9

[12]

Let's choose executors and talk of wills.
And yet not so – for what can we bequeath
Save our deposed bodies to the ground?

Richard II 3.2.148–50

Kings and mightiest potentates must die,
For that's the end of human misery.

1 Henry VI 3.2.134–5

Nothing can we call our own but death.

Richard II 3.2.152

As dead as a doornail.

2 Henry VI 4.10.39

Of all my lands
Is nothing left me but my body's length.
Why, what is pomp, rule, reign, but earth and dust?
And live we how we can, yet die we must.

3 Henry VI 5.2.25–8

The sands are numbered that makes up my life.

3 Henry VI 1.4.25

Here burns my candle out.

3 Henry VI 2.6.1

He that dies pays all debts.

Tempest 3.2.132

Doomsday is near; die all, die merrily.

1 Henry IV 4.1.134

No further, sir; a man may rot even here.

King Lear 5.2.8

Beat not the bones of the buried. When he breathed,
he was a man.

Love's Labour's Lost 5.2.660–1

Lambkins, we will live.

Henry V 2.1.126

RESIGNATION

I have a journey, sir, shortly to go;
My master calls me, I must not say no.

King Lear 5.3.320–1

A man can die but once, we owe God a death.

2 Henry IV 3.2.233–4

More are men's ends marked than their lives before.
The setting sun, and music at the close,
As the last taste of sweets, is sweetest last,
Writ in remembrance more than things long past.

Richard II 2.1.11–14

Death, a necessary end,
Will come when it will come.

Julius Caesar 2.2.36–7

Duncan is in his grave;
After life's fitful fever he sleeps well.

Macbeth 3.2.22–3

Be absolute for death: either death or life
Shall thereby be the sweeter.

Measure for Measure 3.1.5–6

The worst is death, and death will have his day.

Richard II 3.2.103

[17]

CONTEMPLATING DEATH

To be, or not to be, that is the question:
Whether 'tis nobler in the mind to suffer
The slings and arrows of outrageous fortune,
Or to take arms against a sea of troubles
And by opposing end them. To die – to sleep,
No more; and by a sleep to say we end
The heart-ache and the thousand natural shocks
That flesh is heir to: 'tis a consummation
Devoutly to be wished. To die, to sleep;
To sleep, perchance to dream – ay, there's the rub:
For in that sleep of death what dreams may come,
When we have shuffled off this mortal coil,
Must give us pause – there's the respect
That makes calamity of so long life.
For who would bear the whips and scorns of time,
Th'oppressor's wrong, the proud man's contumely,
The pangs of disprized love, the law's delay,
The insolence of office, and the spurns
That patient merit of th'unworthy takes,
When he himself might his quietus make
With a bare bodkin? Who would fardels bear,
To grunt and sweat under a weary life,

But that the dread of something after death,
The undiscovered country, from whose bourn
No traveller returns, puzzles the will,
And makes us rather bear those ills we have
Than fly to others that we know not of?
Thus conscience does make cowards of us all.

Hamlet 3.1.56–83

O that this too too sullied flesh would melt,
Thaw and resolve itself into a dew,
Or that the Everlasting had not fixed
His canon 'gainst self-slaughter.

Hamlet 1.2.129–32

Every bondman in his own hand bears
The power to cancel his captivity.

Julius Caesar 1.3.101–2

A man that apprehends death no more dreadfully but as a drunken sleep; careless, reckless, and fearless of what's past, present, or to come: insensible of mortality, and desperately mortal.

Measure for Measure 4.2.142–5

Ay, but to die, and go we know not where;
To lie in cold obstruction, and to rot;
This sensible warm motion to become
A kneaded clod; and the delighted spirit
To bath in fiery floods, or to reside
In thrilling region of thick-ribbed ice;
To be imprisoned in the viewless winds
And blown with restless violence round about
The pendent world.

Measure for Measure 3.1.117–25

World-Weariness

By my troth Nerissa, my little body is aweary of this great world.

Merchant of Venice 1.2.1–2

      O God! God!
How weary, stale, flat, and unprofitable
Seem to me all the uses of this world!
Fie on't, ah fie, 'tis an unweeded garden
That grows to seed; things rank and gross in nature
Possess it merely.

Hamlet 1.2.132–7

I 'gin to be aweary of the sun,
And wish th'estate o'th' world were now undone.

Macbeth 5.5.49–50

There's nothing in this world can make me joy:
Life is as tedious as a twice-told tale
Vexing the dull ear of a drowsy man.

King John 3.3.107–9

I hold the world but as the world . . .
A stage, where every man must play a part,
And mine a sad one.

Merchant of Venice 1.1.77–9

We have no friend
But resolution and the briefest end.

Antony and Cleopatra 4.15.94–5

POLONIUS My lord, I will take my leave of you.
HAMLET You cannot, sir, take from me anything that
I will not more willingly part withal – except my life,
except my life, except my life.

Hamlet 2.2.213–17

Had I but died an hour before this chance,
I had lived a blessed time; for, from this instant,
There's nothing serious in mortality;
All is but toys: renown, and grace, is dead;
The wine of life is drawn, and the mere lees
Is left this vault to brag of.

Macbeth 2.3.89–94

SEYTON The Queen, my Lord, is dead.
MACBETH She should have died hereafter:
There would have been a time for such a word.
Tomorrow, and tomorrow, and tomorrow,
Creeps in this petty pace from day to day,
To the last syllable of recorded time;
And all our yesterdays have lighted fools
The way to dusty death. Out, out, brief candle!
Life's but a walking shadow; a poor player,
That struts and frets his hour upon the stage,
And then is heard no more: it is a tale
Told by an idiot, full of sound and fury,
Signifying nothing.

Macbeth 5.5.16–28

As flies to wanton boys are we to the gods,
They kill us for their sport.

King Lear 4.1.38–9

Dying Words

The tongues of dying men
Inforce attention like deep harmony.

Richard II 2.1.5–6

If thou didst ever hold me in thy heart,
Absent thee from felicity awhile,
And in this harsh world draw thy breath in pain
To tell my story.

Hamlet 5.2.353–6

The rest is silence.

Hamlet 5.2.365

I am dying, Egypt, dying. Only
I here importune death awhile until
Of many thousand kisses the poor last
I lay upon thy lips.

Antony and Cleopatra 4.15.19–22

There is so hot a summer in my bosom,
That all my bowels crumble up to dust:
I am a scribbled form, drawn with a pen
Upon a parchment, and against this fire
Do I shrink up.

King John 5.7.30–4

Heaven take my soul, and England keep my bones!

King John 4.3.10

Pray you undo this button.

King Lear 5.3.308

Now my soul hath elbow-room.

King John 5.7.28

An old man, broken with the storms of state,
Is come to lay his weary bones among ye.
Give him a little earth, for charity.

Henry VIII 4.2.21–3

Et tu, Brute?

Julius Caesar 3.1.77

Soft you, a word or two before you go.
I have done the state some service, and they know't:
No more of that. I pray you, in your letters,
When you shall these unlucky deeds relate,
Speak of me as I am. Nothing extenuate,
Nor set down aught in malice. Then must you speak
Of one that loved not wisely, but too well;
Of one not easily jealous, but being wrought,
Perplexed in the extreme; of one whose hand,
Like the base Indian, threw a pearl away
Richer than all his tribe.

Othello 5.2.338–48

Unarm, Eros. The long day's task is done
And we must sleep.

Antony and Cleopatra 4.14.35–6

Farewells

Come, I'll be friends with thee, Jack, thou art going to the wars, and whether I shall ever see thee again or no there is nobody cares.

2 Henry IV 2.4.63–6

Whether we shall meet again, I know not:
Therefore our everlasting farewell take.

Julius Caesar 5.1.114–15

The last of all the Romans, fare thee well.

Julius Caesar 5.3.99

So part we sadly in this troublous world,
To meet with joy in sweet Jerusalem.

3 Henry VI 5.5.7–8

As many farewells as be stars in heaven,
With distinct breath and consigned kisses to them,
[Time] fumbles up into a loose adieu
And scants us with a single famished kiss,
Distasted with the salt of broken tears.

Troilus and Cressida 4.4.43–7

Good night, ladies, good night. Sweet ladies,
good night, good night.

Hamlet 4.5.72–3

Grief

Cry, Trojans, cry!

Troilus and Cressida 2.2.97

O, grief and time,
Fearful consumers, you will all devour!

Two Noble Kinsmen 1.1.69–70

Honest plain words best pierce the ear of grief.

Love's Labour's Lost 5.2.749

Every one can master a grief but he that has it.

Much Ado About Nothing 3.2.26–7

My grief lies onward, and my joy behind.

Sonnet 50

I have that within which passes show,
These but the trappings and the suits of woe.

Hamlet 1.2.85–6

My grief lies all within,
And these external manners of lament
Are merely shadows to the unseen grief
That swells with silence in the tortured soul.

Richard II 4.1.295–8

Sorrow breaks seasons and reposing hours,
Makes the night morning, and the noontide night.

Richard III 1.4.76–7

Tell me what blessings I have here alive,
That I should fear to die.

Winter's Tale 3.2.106–7

Time will come and take my love away.
  This thought is as a death, which cannot choose
  But weep to have that which it fears to lose.

Sonnet 64

Grief fills the room up of my absent child,
Lies in his bed, walks up and down with me,
Puts on his pretty looks, repeats his words,
Remembers me of all his gracious parts,
Stuffs out his vacant garments with his form.

King John 3.3.93–7

MACDUFF He has no children. – All my pretty ones?
Did you say all? – O Hell-kite! – All?
What, all my pretty chickens, and their dam,
At one fell swoop?
MALCOLM Dispute it like a man.
MACDUFF   I shall do so;
But I must also feel it as a man:
I cannot but remember such things were,
That were most precious to me.

Macbeth 4.3.216–23

O you gods!
Why do you make us love your goodly gifts,
And snatch them straight away?

Pericles 3.1.22–4

Howl, howl, howl, howl! O, you are men of stones!
Had I your tongues and eyes, I'd use them so
That heaven's vault should crack: she's gone for ever.

King Lear 5.3.255–7

And my poor fool is hanged. No, no, no life!
Why should a dog, a horse, a rat have life
And thou no breath at all?

King Lear 5.3.304–6

Cease; thou know'st
He dies to me again, when talked of.

Winter's Tale 5.1.118–1

Give sorrow words; the grief, that does not speak,
Whispers the o'er-fraught heart, and bids it break.

Macbeth 4.3.209–10

Moderate lamentation is the right of the dead;
excessive grief the enemy to the living.

All's Well That Ends Well 1.1.54–5

My old heart is cracked, it's cracked.

King Lear 2.1.90

Day doth daily draw my sorrows longer,
And night doth nightly make grief's length seem stronger.

Sonnet 28

VIOLA What country, friends, is this?
CAPTAIN This is Illyria, lady.
VIOLA And what should I do in Illyria?
My brother he is in Elysium.

Twelfth Night 1.2.1–4

What's gone and what's past help
Should be past grief.

Winter's Tale 3.2.220–1

Elegies

Now cracks a noble heart. Good night, sweet prince,
And flights of angels sing thee to thy rest.

Hamlet 5.2.367–8

His legs bestrid the ocean; his reared arm
Crested the world; his voice was propertied
As all the tuned spheres, and that to friends;
But when he meant to quail and shake the orb,
He was as rattling thunder. For his bounty,
There was no winter in't: an autumn it was
That grew the more by reaping. His delights
Were dolphin-like: they showed his back above
The element they lived in. In his livery
Walked crowns and crownets; realms and islands were
As plates dropped from his pocket.

Antony and Cleopatra 5.2.81–91

If you have tears, prepare to shed them now.

Julius Caesar 3.2.167

Beauty, truth and rarity,
Grace in all simplicity,
Here enclosed, in cinders lie.

Phoenix and Turtle 53–5

Now boast thee, Death, in thy possession lies
A lass unparalleled.

Antony and Cleopatra 5.2.313–14

This was the noblest Roman of them all.

Julius Caesar 5.5.68

The crown o'th' earth doth melt . . .
O withered is the garland of the war,
The soldier's pole is fallen; young boys and girls
Are level now with men; the odds is gone
And there is nothing left remarkable
Beneath the visiting moon.

Antony and Cleopatra 4.15.65–70

A terrible childbed hast thou had, my dear;
No light, no fire: th'unfriendly elements
Forgot thee utterly; nor have I time
To give thee hallowed to thy grave, but straight
Must cast thee, scarcely coffined, in the ooze;
Where, for a monument upon thy bones,
And e'er-remaining lamps, the belching whale
And humming water must o'erwhelm thy corpse,
Lying with simple shells.

Pericles 3.1.56–64

Like as the waves make towards the pebbled shore,
So do our minutes hasten to their end,
Each changing place with that which goes before,
In sequent toil all forwards do contend.
Nativity, once in the main of light,
Crawls to maturity; wherewith being crowned
Crooked eclipses 'gainst his glory fight,
And time, that gave, doth now his gift confound.
Time doth transfix the flourish set on youth,
And delves the parallels in beauty's brow;
Feeds on the rarities of nature's truth,
And nothing stands but for his scythe to mow.
    And yet to times in hope my verse shall stand,
    Praising thy worth, despite his cruel hand.

Sonnet 60

Alas, poor Yorick. I knew him, Horatio,
a fellow of infinite jest, of most excellent fancy.

Hamlet 5.1.182–3

Or I shall live, your epitaph to make;
Or you survive, when I in earth am rotten;
From hence your memory death cannot take,
Although in me each part will be forgotten.
Your name from hence immortal life shall have,
Though I, once gone, to all the world must die;
The earth can yield me but a common grave,
When you entombed in men's eyes shall lie.
Your monument shall be my gentle verse,
Which eyes not yet created shall o'er-read,
And tongues to be your being shall rehearse,
When all the breathers of this world are dead.
   You still shall live, such virtue hath my pen,
   Where breath most breathes, even in the mouths of men.

Sonnet 81

I would give you some violets, but they withered all
when my father died.

Hamlet 4.5.181–3

Graves

Come away, come away death,
And in sad cypress let me be laid.
Fie away, fie away breath,
I am slain by a fair cruel maid:
 My shroud of white, stuck all with yew,
  O prepare it.
 My part of death no one so true
  Did share it.

Not a flower, not a flower sweet,
On my black coffin let there be strewn:
Not a friend, not a friend greet
My poor corpse, where my bones shall be thrown:
 A thousand thousand sighs to save,
  Lay me, O where
 Sad true lover never find my grave,
  To weep there.

Twelfth Night 2.4.51–66

Fear no more the heat o'th' sun,
    Nor the furious winter's rages,
Thou thy worldly task has done,
    Home art gone and ta'en thy wages.
Golden lads and girls all must,
As chimney-sweepers, come to dust.

Fear no more the frown o'th' great,
    Thou art past the tyrant's stroke,
Care no more to clothe and eat,
    To thee the reed is as the oak:
The sceptre, learning, physic, must
All follow this and come to dust.

Fear no more the lightning-flash.
    Nor th' all-dreaded thunder-stone.
Fear not slander, censure rash.
    Thou hast finished joy and moan.
All lovers young, all lovers must
Consign to thee and come to dust.

No exorciser harm thee!
Nor no witchcraft charm thee!
Ghost unlaid forbear thee!
Nothing ill come near thee!
Quiet consummation have,
And renowned be thy grave!

Cymbeline 4.2.258–81

Everything that grows
Holds in perfection but a little moment.

Sonnet 15

Lay her i'th' earth,
And from her fair and unpolluted flesh
May violets spring.

Hamlet 5.1.236–8

With wild wood-leaves and weeds I ha' strewed his grave
And on it said a century of prayers.

Cymbeline 4.2.390–1

The ground that gave them first has them again:
Their pleasures here are past, so is their pain.

Cymbeline 4.2.289–90

Endings

Since brass, nor stone, nor earth, nor boundless sea,
But sad mortality o'er-sways their power,
How with this rage shall beauty hold a plea,
Whose action is no stronger than a flower?

Sonnet 65

So quick bright things come to confusion.

Midsummer Night's Dream 1.1.149

What's past and what's to come is strewed with husks
And formless ruin of oblivion.

Troilus and Cressida 4.5.167–8

All that lives must die,
Passing through nature to eternity.

Hamlet 1.2.72–3

Let time shape, and there an end.

2 Henry IV 3.2.326–7

The end crowns all.

Troilus and Cressida 4.5.224

We are such stuff
As dreams are made on, and our little life
Is rounded with a sleep.

Tempest 4.1.156–8

[48]